**Forward:**

Our ancestors lived interesting lives from all over the globe. They were brave and strong and helped create this country of America. It is important to know where we come from, what our ancestors did and the sacrifices they made for us. I encourage everyone to pass this information on to future generations.

Since this information is taken from many different sources and public records there are always discrepancies in dates and/or spelling of names. This is the most accurate information I can find on the England, McKinney and Little family lines. However it is not always 100 percent accurate.

**DEDICATION:** To all my England and McKinney ancestors.

**CONTENTS:**

**England Family – Page 1**
**McKinney Family – Page 21**
**Little Family – Page 35**

# THE

# ENGLAND

# FAMILY

## THE ENGLAND FAMILY

My England family came from Dorset England to Ireland to NC to Burke County, NC to White County, TN (Sparta) and on to West Tennessee. They were in Putnam County, Decatur County and Henderson County, TN. They were large land owners. Other England family members first settled in Massachusetts and Maryland. We also have connections to the England's who moved to Texas and Illinois.

The England family was first found in Norfolk, England where they held a family seat before the Norman Conquest and the arrival of Duke William at Hastings in 1066 A.D. The name England comes from the early history of Britain, specifically the Anglo Saxons. It is from the fact that they lived in a meadow beside water. The surname England originally derived from the Old English word Engelond which referred to a meadow beside a rushing river. The recorded variations of the England name include Englund, Englend. The England's were found in early American records. John England was one of the founders of Charlestown, Massachusetts in 1620

**Places where Our England's lived:**

Dorset England
Gloucestershire, England
Devon England
Donegal Ireland
Burke County, NC
White Co, TN
Decatur Co TN
Henderson Co, TN
Williamson County, IL
Hunt County, TX

**Dr. John McCallister England**
B: 1827 Henderson Co, TN
M:
D: 1863 Illinois, USA

**Avenette Ross England**
B: 1793 Burke, NC
D: 1883 Arkansas, USA

**Martha Middleton**
B: 1802 South Carolina
D: 1864

**Ammon / Aaron England**
B: 1856 Putnam, TN
M:
D: Putnam, TN

**James Hanna**
B: 1799
D: 1867

**Rebecca Hanna**
B: 1829 Sardis, TN
M:
D: 1919 Greenville, Texas, USA

**Ellender Courtney**
B: 1800
D: 1884

**James Leslie England**
B: 13 Dec 1885 Sardis, TN
M:
D: Jan 1972 Sardis, TN

**Margaret White**
B: 1857 Sardis, TN
M:
D: 1902 Decatur, TN

**Margaret Ruth England**
B: 28 Jan 1918 Sardis, TN
M:
D: 22 Sept 1978 Jackson, TN

**William McKinney**
B: 1847 Decatur, TN
M:
D:

**Mary McKinney**
B: 1888 Sardis, TN
M:
D: 1981 Sardis, TN

**Mary Jane Reynolds**
B: 1856 TN
M:
D:

4

**William England**
B: 1710 Donegal, Ireland
M:
D: 1800 Burke, NC

**William W England**
B: 1679 Donegal, Ireland
D: 1711 New Kent, VA

**Mary Anderson**
B: 1674 New Kent, VA
D: 1710 Virginia, USA

**John England**
B: 1730 Donegal, Ireland
M:
D: 1795 Burke, NC

**Mary Watson**
B: 1724 New Jersey
M:
D: 1790 Georgia, USA

**William Watson**
B: 1706
D:

**Sarah**
B: 1692
D:

**John England**
B: 1765 Burke, NC
M:
D: 1825 Madison County, Missouri, USA

**Jane Ann Grant**
B: 1738
M:
D: 1779

**Avenette Ross England**
B: 1793 Burke, NC
M:
D: 1883 Arkansas City, Arkansas, Arkansas, US

**Margaret Ross**
B:
M:
D:

**Richard England**
B: 1540 Gloucestershire, England
D:

**John England**
B: 1580 England
M:
D:

**Nicholas England**
B: 1604 Devon, England
M:
D: 1632 England

**John England**
B: 1624 Dorset, England
M:
D: Dorset, England

**Mary Lippincott**
B:
M:
D:

**William W England**
B: 1679 Donegal, Ireland
M:
D: 1711 New Kent, VA

**GENERATION ONE:**
the author Katherine Fletcher

**GENERATION TWO:**
Margaret Anita Rice – author's mother

**GENERATION THREE:**
Margaret Ruth England 1918-1978 Sardis, TN to Jackson, TN and Oral Holland Rice (1911-1993)

**GENERATION FOUR:**
James Leslie England 1884-1972 Sardis, TN
married Mary Estelle McKinney (1888-1910) - her parents William McKinney and Mary Jane Reynolds

**GENERATION FIVE:**
Ammon England 1856 Putnam, TN Died Harrison, Missouri
married Margaret White (1857--1902) Sardis, TN to Decatur, TN

**GENERATION SIX:**
Dr. John McCallister England (1827-1863) and Rebecca Hanna (1829-1919)
Henderson Co, TN to Williamson Co, IL    and Sardis, TN to Greenville, TX

**GENERATION SEVEN:**
Avenette Ross England (1793-1883) and Martha Middleton (1802-1864)
Burke County, NC

**GENERATION EIGHT**
John England (1765-1825) and Margaret Ross
Burke County, NC to Madison Co, Missouri

**GENERATION NINE:**
John England (1730 Donegal, Ireland to 1795 Burke, NC) married Jane Ann Grant (1738-1779)

**GENERATION TEN:**
William England (1710 Donegal, Ireland to 1800 Burke, NC) married Mary Watson (1713-1790)

**GENERATION ELEVEN:**
William W. England (1679 Donegal, Ireland to 1711 New Kent, VA) married Mary Anderson

**GENERATION TWELVE:**
John England (1624 Dorset, England to 1724) and Anne Mary Martin (1626-1685)

**GENERATION THIRTEEN:**
Nicholas England (1604-1632) Devon England and Mary Lippincott

**GENERATION FOURTEEN**
John England (1580-) Born in Marshfield Gloucestershire, England

**GENERATION FIFTEEN**
Richard England (1540-1604)
Born in Marshfield Gloucestershire, England.  Died in Cowley, Gloucestershire, England.

**Generation One** – the author Katherine Fletcher

**Generation Two** – Margaret Anita Rice

**Generation Three**

Margaret Ruth England 1918-1978 Sardis, TN to Jackson, TN and Oral Holland Rice (1911-1993)

Their Children:

Linda Rice
Mickey Rice
Margaret Anita Rice

My grandmother Ruth England Rice was a great woman and raised three wonderful daughters. Her husband, my grandfather was Holland Rice. They lived in Sardis, TN, Savannah, TN and Memphis, TN. They were wonderful humans with big hearts and were helpful to everyone they encountered. More information about Ruth England and Holland Rice can be found in my Rice Family History Book.

Ruth England Rice and Holland Rice

Ruth England Rice with the Fletcher grandchildren

**Generation Four**

**James Leslie England and Mary Estelle McKinney**

James Leslie England (12-13-1884 in Sardis, TN) to 01-1972 Sardis, TN
married Mary McKinney (1888-1981) married in 1910 in Henderson Co, TN.

Mary McKinney's parents were William McKinney and Mary Jane Reynolds. Her siblings were Annie C, James W, Charles L, Lura M., Mary E, Lina E., Kenny, Claude E, Murtle E.

James was listed in the 1920 census in Decatur Co and the 1930 census in Henderson County, TN. These are right next to each other. He also served in World War I at the age of 33 in September of 1918. He was living in Bath Springs in Decatur Co at the time. He was also married by then. He was a farmer.

In the 1900 census he is 14 years old and living with his father Ammon and mother Margaret (this is Margaret White). His siblings are listed as William, Rebecca, Cora, James, Noah, Millie, Jewell and Ida.

In 1910 he was with Mary (wife), Opal and Johnnie (children) in Decatur Co, TN. His neighbors included England relatives Annie, Sarah, Mah, Carrie Smith, Mefie England, wife and children as well as several White families. The White's were related to James Leslie's grandmother's family. (Margaret White / Ammon England).

In 1920 he was still living in Decatur Co, TN with wife Mary and children, Opal, Jimmie, Irene, Willie A, and Ruth. The other England and White relatives were not living next to them.

In 1930 they were living in Henderson Co, TN with wife Mary and children Irene, Robert, Willie and Ruth. Living on the same street are many White relatives and Ray Little.

Their Children:

**Margaret Ruth England** (1918-1978) My grandmother whom everyone called Ruth. Married Holland Oral Rice and had 3 daughters: Linda, Mickey, Anita

Irene – (1-18-1912 to 12-22-2010) my wonderful Great aunt Irene who makes the best biscuits in the whole world.  She was my substitute Grandmother after her sister Ruth (my Grandmother) died when I was a teenager.  She has always been a huge part of our family and well loved by all.  She died in 2010 and will be greatly missed.  She married Jones Holt.
    * See Aunt Irene's Secret Southern Recipes Book at the end of this book.

Robert – married Ann Murley and was in the World war.  Had a son Les.

Opal 1906-1961 – played on the Sardis girls basketball team. She married Aubert Little. Had children: Gary, Larry, Jimmie ("Budgy")

 ** See The Little Genealogy at the end of this book.

Jimmie England 1909-1995 - married Clyde Carter Little - worked at Sardis P.O. and Memphis as the assistant postmaster.  Had sons, Pat, Tim and Stan Little.  She died of cancer at 86 years old. She played on the girl's basketball team in Sardis, TN.

* See the Little genealogy at the end of this book **

William A. (1915-1972)  Called Bill and died of a brain tumor in his old age. Bill worked with Clyde Little in his cattle business for years.

James Leslie England and Mary McKinney England

Left to Right: Irene England, Mary McKinney England, Robert, James Leslie England, Ruth England Rice, Jimmie England

Irene England Holt

**Generation Five**
**Ammon M. England (1855-1937) and Margaret A. White (1854-)**
Ammon died in Bemis, TN (Madison Co, TN)

Their Children:

William Franklin. (1875-1954) married Anner Ella Young

Rebecca A. (1879-1953) married Eugene Alonzo Wyatt

Ammon M. (1881)

Cora E. (1883-1968) married George Calvin Simmons

**James L. (1885) married Mary McKinney**

Ida M. (1887)

Noah V. (1883)

Millie V (1883)


**Generation Six**
**Dr. John McAllister England (1827-1880) and Rebecca March Hanna (1829-1919)**

In 1827 John lived in Sardis, TN. In 1860 still living in Henderson Co, TN and 1864 died in Williamston, Illinois.

Rebecca Hanna comes from a well known family. Her father was James Hanna (1799-1867) and her mother Ellender Courtney (1806-1884).

Captain James Hanna was born in Kentucky and his parents were John Hanna (SC 1772) and Rebecca Cunningham. Rebecca was born in Sardis, TN and died in 1919 in Greenville, Hunt County, Texas. After the death of Dr. John England, her husband she returned to Sardis I 1865 where the family lived until 1871 when they moved to Greenville, Texas. Rebecca also married James Allred and had a son Calvin.

Before the Civil war, Captain James Hanna provided a way station near where Springhill Cemetery now is. There was a stage coach road from a settlement that is now Bolivar by way of the small settlement of Sardis to Clifton on Tennessee River. He would provide food and water for horses and stables where they could groom their horses. He also provided bed and board for a night for the people.

In fact the Hannabilt truck bed was made by Rebecca Hanna's relatives. A rather unique business had been established in 1934 by J. T. Hanna. He had a woodworking shop where he built cedar chests, cabinets, swings and once he even made a cedar bed. Someone asked him to make a truck bed and thereby opened a new avenue to a bigger job. From this beginning he built truck beds for people all over West Tennessee and northern Mississippi. He made about twenty for one company in New Jersey. He had an unusual trademark -- Hannabilt. W. H. McBride, one of our local boys who was in the Army in World War II, said he was in Denver, Colorado, and there saw a Hannabilt truck bed. In 1944, Mr. Hanna started a hardware store. In 1949, the town of Sardis was incorporated and J. T. Hanna was the first mayor.

Their Children:

**Ammon England (1855) married Margaret White**

Annabel (1847-1934) born in Sardis, died in Greenville, Texas

Martha Ellen (1847-1934) died in Dallas, TX married William G. Craig

John Frank (1848-1925) born in Sardis, died in Sulphur, Oklahoma

James Avanant (1850-1939) – married May Ann Stout (1856-1934). They were married over 50 years. After living in TX, James returned to Decaturville and lived with his aunt and uncle, Adeline and Duncan Kennedy. He taught school and studied law and was admitted to the bar ion 1877. He was also the Clerk of the Chancery Court. He was one of the founders of the Decatur County Bank in 1899. He also was a special judge of the old 12th judicial circuit court. Mary Ann was born in Perryville, TN to William and Jane Coats Stout. Mary Ann was a Decatur Co Elementary School teacher for over 30 years. Their daughter Nelle England Dunivant was one the first women appointed clerk and master of the Chancery Court in the whole state of TN.

> The grandson of James Avant (above) was James Stout England who married Tennessee Belle Yarbro. James was a lawyer and attended Notre Dame and Northwestern University. During World War II he volunteered for the Navy. He participated in several invasions in New Guinea, Admiralty Islands and the Philippines. He was awarded 8 battle stars and the Bronze Star!

Mary Carolina (1852) born in Sardis, died in Greenville Texas

Alfred Alexandrian (1854-1921) born in Sardis, died in Greenville, TX

Rebecca Elizabeth (1858-) born in Sardis, died in Greenville, TX

Randall S. (1860-1861) – born in Sardis,

George (1862)

John McCallister – (1864)

**Generation Seven**:

**Avenette Ross England (1793-1883) Burke, NC and Martha Middleton (1802-1864)**
They married in 1820 in Maury County, TN.

Martha Middleton was from SC.

In 1850 there were in Henderson County, TN.  In 1860 lived in Decatur Co, TN.
Avenette died in Arkansas City, Arkansas in 1883.

Their Children:

Franklin (1821) born in TN,

**John McCallister (1827-1864) married Rebecca Hanna**

George Henderson (1828-1880) born and died in Henderson County, TN

Avanant Ross (1833-1907) born in Anderson TN, died in Hunt Co, TX

Mary Isabelle (1835-1915) born in TN, died in Wolfe City, TX

Martha L. (1837-

Miranda Adaline (1841-1935) born in TN, died in Hunt County, TX

Nancy R. (1844) born in TN, married _____ Pittman.


**Generation Eight**

**John (1765 Burke, NC to 1825 Madison Co, Missouri) married Margaret Ross**
In 1790.  Had previous wife Elizabeth Howard who he married.

**Their Children:**

John (1785-1841) born in Pennsylvania, died Burke Co., NC or Missouri.  Their children were born in Rutherford Co, TN as well as Bedford Co and White Co, TN.

**Avenette Ross (1793-1883) who married Martha Middleton**

James Ross (1809-1866) married Margaret McCormack and most of his children were born in Missouri.

Enos

Jane – married _____ Brooks and later married ___ Creecie

Rebecca (1795)

John


**Generation Nine**

**John England  DOB: 1730-1738 Donegal, Ireland DOD: 03-16-1795 Burke, NC**
**married Jane Grant  DOB: 1738 Tyrone, Ireland and DOD: 1779 Burke, NC**

John was a private in the Revolutionary War in Burke Co, NC.
They had 11 children.   North Carolina Rev. Soldiers, Sailors, Patriots & Descendents book.


England, John (R-Pvt-NC) c 1730 - 1795
m. Ann Grant
\*\*\*\*\*\*\*\*\*\*\*\*\*\*\*\*\*\*\*\*\*\*\*
From "History of White County Tennessee"
The John England family is so intertwined with other families in White County, especially the Scott's that this article will hit highlights only with no real depth and many names will be omitted. For more complete information, refer to published books and materials in the White County Library on the England family.

John England, born in County Donegal, Ireland about 1730, was of Irish, Scotch, and English decent. He was married to Jane Anne Grant, born in county Tyrone, Ireland about 1738. John emigrated from Ireland to Wilmington, NC about 1750 and settled on the Haw River. Later he moved presumably to Burke Co., NC. He served as a private in the Revolutionary War. He was a farmer and a Quaker. John's Will was signed in Burke Co., NC on March 16, 1775. His brother Daniel was named executor of his will. John died in 1775 in Burke Co., NC. It is believed that the England family came to America with the Grant and Ross families, that they landed in Wilmington, NC and they settled on the Hawes River. , about 1750. John England was a Revolutionary soldier. He was a Quaker, a farmer, and it has been said that he was half Irish, one-fourth English, and one-fourth Scott.

Jane's father was Col. Jesse Grant and her mother Jean Bumes.
Jane Grant's grandfather was in Grant's field and fought the famous Cowpen's Battle. One of the family, Col. Grant, was in Active service all during the Revolutionary War, was in Mabanes Division. The father of Col. Grant was killed by Mr. Hightower by shooting with a ramrod.  In fact the Battle of Cowpens was fought on England / Grant's land.

Their Children:

      Elizabeth (1758 Burke, NC to 1829 Surrey Co, NC) married Silas Murphy

      **John (1765 Burke, NC to Madison Co, Missouri) married Margaret Ross**

      Rhoda (1773 Burke, NC to 1843 Jackson Co, TN) born in White Co, TN (Sparta)

      Aaron (1760-1838 Burke, NC to 1839 White Co, TN) married Elise Mayberry
          Aaron was the founder of White's County, TN (Sparta) and prominent citizen.

Many England's were in White County and there is England's Cove where many lived. Aaron had several hundred acres of land and was a slave owner.

Aaron England 1760 - 1839 Burke, NC to White Co, TN

One of founders of Sparta, TN

Margaret (1767 Deep River, Burke Co, TN to ?) married Benjamin Harris

Joseph Grant (1774 Burke, NC to Caldeonia Washington Co, Missouri) married
    Mary Reed (or Margaret Ross)

Ezekiel (1760 Burke, NC to 1819 Wilkes Co, NC) married Charlotte Council

Keziah (1770 Burke, NC to 1820 Cathey's Creek Buncombe, NC) married Jonathan
    Duckworth

Sarah (1777 Burkes Co, NC)

Mary Catherine (1784 Burke, NC to 1870 Morgan, Alabama) married Nicodemus
Hackworth

Beersheba (Barsheba)(1779 Burke, NC to after 1850 Greene Co, TN)
    married John McNerk

## WILL OF JOHN ENGLAND

Book of Jared by Eleanor Hall
Pgs. 683684
IN THE Name of God Amen: I, John England of the State of North Carolina and County
of Burke, being sick and weak of body, but of sound mind and memory and calling to
mind the Mortality of My body and that it is appointed to all Men once to die: Do
continue this my last will and testament & earnestly disior that it May bee Received as
such - IMPRESS My Soal I bequeth to almighty God that gave it humbly beseeching His Most
gracious acceptance of it through the Merrit & meditation of Jesus Christ and My body
to the Earth from whence it Came to bee discreetly Intred therar in at the discretion of
My beloved Wife & Exacitors hearafter nameid.
And as to the worldly goods whearwith it has pleased God to bless mee I give and
bequeath as followith, Viz: All my debts being first paid, I give & bequith to my beloved
wife a good horse (s)adil and bridil, a Cowe and Calf, & a good fethor bead and a Jenteel
living cut of the estate as long as shee Remains My widow.
ITEM: I give & bequeath to my Eldest sun, Aron England ten pounds and no more ITEM:
I give & bequeath to my Eldest Daughter Elizabeth Murphey one Cow & Calf and
no more -
ITEM: I gave and beqath to my Second daughter Margit Harris one Cow and Calf and no
more -
ITEM: I give & bequeath to my sun John England the tract of Land of 200 Acres that I
bought of William Welch when he comes to the age of 21 years, and if it Can bee attained
in the Meantime to be applied to the schooling and Maintaining of him Self & his Mother
and if Required the executors May Sell the Lands and purchase as Mutch in a Sutipill place
for them again and if either of them should die before they Cum of eage ther tract of Land
to be sold and divided among the Rest of my Suns then a living -
ITEM: and all the rest of My Estate of Stock horses Cattill & hogs or whatsoever else Not
mentioned of My property May Equally divided among the Rest of My Children VIZ:
Marey, Rhoda, Kezziah, Sarah, Barsheba, John & Josiph England Shear and have alike -
I do hereby nominate & appoint my sun Aron England & My beloved Brother Daniel
England my Executors of this my last will and testament and I do by these presents
Disanull all othor Will or Wils heretobore by mee mad or Rittin in WITNESS whereof I
have hereonto Sot my hand and affixed my sail this 16 day of March - 1795.
And my Lott in town that is to bee soald and divided amongst these that is to have an
aquill part of What is yet to bee Divid
John England (Sail)
State of No. Carolina Court of Pleas & quarter sessions Burke County
October Term 1795
From: North Carolina Historical Commission Burke County Wills
ENGLAND

## Generation Ten

**William England (1710 Donegal, Ireland to 1800 Burke, NC)**
married Elizabeth Wilcox (1710-1735) and died at 35 years old. They had one child named
William. He later married Mary Watson (1713-1790)
Mary Watson died in Chesterfield, PA.

Their Children were:

William (mother Elizabeth Wilcox)

**John 1733 Donegal, Ireland to 03-16-1795 Burke, NC married Jane Ann Grant. (mother is Elizabeth Wilcox)**

Joseph 1736 Donegal, Ireland to 1831 Habersham Co, Georgia.  married Charity Cole (mother Elizabeth Wilcox)

Clara 1743 in NC  married William Michel

Samuel 1740

Daniel - 1752 Maryland to 09-09-1816 Burke Co, NC .  married Margaret Guin

**According to the book "England-McVay and Descendants" written by ClaraHodge, William's family originated in England, went to Ireland during the Great Emigration, came to America with his parents to Maryland then moved to Pennsylvania in 1733. He married Elizabeth Wilcox in Chester Co, PA and they had one son William England Jr.  He arrived in NC in 1760. William lived in Fayetteville,NC in 1790 with his brother-in-law John Wilcox.  He later married Mary Watson of New Jersey.   They moved to NC in 1760 and William obtained a grant of land in Chattam County, NC.  Elizabeth's parents were Thomas Wilcox.  Mary Watson's father was William Watson of New Jersey and Mother, Elizabeth Cole.

It was in North Carolina that William England went into partnership with his brother-in-law, John Wilcox, and built an iron foundry.  The iron furnace cast cannons and cannon balls used in the war effort during the Revolution.  Daniel England worked with his father in the foundry on Hunting Creek near Morganton, NC.  He applied for and received deferment from induction into the military because of his work at the foundry.

Daniel died in 1818 in Burke County, NC.  He was recognized by Sons of the American Revolution for his material assistance in the Revolutionary War effort.


**Generation Eleven**

 **William W. England (1679 Donegal, Ireland to 1711 New Kent, VA) married Mary Anderson**

Their children:

John (1700-1768)
Elizabeth (1702-
**William (1710-1800) and Mary Watson**

**Generation Twelve**

**John England (1624 Dorset, England to 1724) and Anne Mary Martin (1626-1685)**

Born in St. Peters Parish, Dorset England and died in 1685 in Burstock, Dorset England. Married 1643.

Their Children:

> John (1640)
> Elizabeth (1644)
> Anne (1651)
> Elizabeth (1657)
> Pascha (1657-1729)
> **William W. (1679-1711) and Mary Anderson**


**Generation Thirteen**
**Nicholas England (1604-1632) Devon England**
and Mary Lippincott

Born in Sydburry, Devon England and died in

**Generation Fourteen**
**John England (1580-)**
Born in Marshfield Gloucestershire, England

Children:

> Nicholas England married Mary Lippincott

**Generation Fifteen**
**Richard England (1540-1604)**
Born in Marshfield Gloucestershire, England.  Died in Cowley, Gloucestershire, England.

Children:
> John England (1580)

# MCKINNEY

# FAMILY

# GENEALOGY

**PLACES WHERE McKINNEY's LIVED:**

It all started in Isle of Skye, Scotland where the genealogy goes back to 1126.
We also have German, Netherlands and Brazil through the wives of the McKinney men.
An interesting mix of cultures and bloodline.

Isle of Skye, Scotland
Donegal and Kerry, Ireland
New Jersey
Pennsylvania
Chester, South Carolina (also known as Anson, NC)
One branch to went to McKinney, Texas, another branch went to Lincoln, KY.
Rockbridge, VA
Decatur Co, TN
Henderson and Hardin Co, TN

The Lincoln CO, KY branch is also the site of McKinney's Fort which was built in the late 1770's. It is the first permanent trading post in Kentucky which furnished supplies to government troops in the Lincoln Co Militia. It was built by Archibald McKinney on the Hanging Fork River. It was an important stop on the Cumberland Trace which connected Stanford, KY to Nashville, TN. When the railroad was built it was called McKinney's Station and is now called McKinney, KY. Descendants of the New Jersey family came down to Rockbridge County, VA and on to Lincoln, KY Archibald had received a 4,000 acre land grant in Lincoln, Ky and that is why he moved from Rockbridge, VA to KY.

The Texas branch of the McKinney's settled McKinney, Texas and one of the descendants was a signer of Texas Declaration of Independence. Another supposedly fought at the Alamo. One was a participant in the Boston Tea party.

**WARS**

Many McKinney's fought in the Revolutionary War and Civil Wars.

**SCOTLAND HERITAGE**

In Scotland there were many name variations of McKinney such as MacKinney, Kinneir, MacKinnons, MacKenziesÓ and others.
It is believed our McKinney line comes from the MacKenzies.
They were known as Kinnaird in Scotland and can trace their roots to the 12th century.
William de Kiner who lived during 1165-1214 and was alive during the reign of King William I. They were connected to the Abbot of Balmerino, Scotland.
Many believe we belong to the MacKinnon clan, which was strong and goes back to 1100.
Some say it is almost certain be don't belong to the MacKinnon clan.

**William McKinney**
B: 1755 United States
M: 1811
D: 1842 United States

**William Mckinney**
B: abt 1811 South Carolina, USA
M:
D: Arkansas, United States

**William MCKINNEY**
B: 25 Aug 1729 United States,
D: 27 Apr 1785 United States

**Barbara CULP**
B: 1733 United States
D: 1790 United States

**Mary Carter**
B: 1775 United States
M: 1811
D: 6 Apr 1840 United States

**Alexander Carter**
B: 16 Jun 1758 United States
D: 5 Jul 1824 United States

**Anna Minskipe**
B: 1741 Virginia, United States
D: 4 Oct 1842 United States

**William Akin Mckinney**
B: 15 May 1847 Tennessee, United States
M: 17 JAN 1875 Decatur
D: 29 Oct 1923 Tennessee, USA

**Rebecca**
B: 1819 South Carolina, USA
M:
D: 1881 Arkansas, United States

**Mary E Mckinney**
B: Jul 1888 Tennessee
M:
D:

**Mary J reynolds**
B: 30 Dec 1856 Tennessee
M: 17 JAN 1875 Decatur
D: 3 Feb 1945

**John DeKynner**
B: 1601 , , , Scotland
M:
D: , , , Scotland

**Simon DeKynner**
B: 1577 , , , Scotland
D:

**david lochland kinneir**
B: 1626 , , , Scotland
M:
D: abt 1665 Midlothia, Scotland,

**Maud**
B: 1601 , , , Scotland
M:
D: , , , Scotland

**John Cullen McKinney**
B: 1650 Isle Skye, , , Scotland
M: 1675 Scleofsky, , , Scotland
D: 1745 Isle Skye, , , Scotland

**Lancelot Threlkeld**
B: 1435 Melmerby, , , England
M: 16 Jan 1469 , England
D: 22 Apr 1493 , , England

**Henry Threlkeld**
B: 29 Sep 1399 , England
D: 18 Nov 1446

**Margaret Thirkland**
B: 1629 , Ayrshire, , Scotland
M:
D: 1670 , , , Scotland

**Margaret Bromflete**
B: 1436 , Yorkshire, , England
M: 16 Jan 1469 , England
D: 12 Apr 1493 , , England

**Mordecai McKinney**
B: 1685 Isle of the Skye, Scotland
M: 1713 Dutch Ref Ch, Hunterdon,
D: 20 May 1760 Lebanon, Hunterdon, New Jers

**Lander**
B: 1630
M:
D: Skye Isle, Scotland

**Agnes Lander**
B: 1654 Scleofsky, , Skye Isle, Scotland
M: 1675 Scleofsky, , , Scotland
D: 1733 Isle Skye, , , Scotland

**GENERATION ONE:**
Mary Estelle McKinney and James Leslie England

**GENERATION TWO:**
William Akin McKinney and Mary Jane Reynolds
1847-1923 Decatur Co, TN

**GENERATION THREE:**
William McKinney and Rebecca
(1811-1880) born in North Carolina / South Carolina (Chester), moved to Henderson Co., TN and died in Arkansas

**GENERATION FOUR:**
William McKinney (1755-1842) and Mary Carter (1775-1840)
Born and died in Chester, SC and Mary born and died in Chester SC

**GENERATION FIVE:**
William McKinney and Barbara Culp
(1729-1785) Born in Rariten, NJ and died in Chester, SC

**GENERATION SIX:**
John Mordecai McKinney (1685-1760) and Marietje Sebring (1685-1760)
He was born in Isle of The Skye, Scotland (or USA), lived in Pennsylvania and New Jersey and died in Lebanon, NJ.

**GENERATION SEVEN:**
John Cullen McKinney (1650-1745) and Agnes Lander (1654-1733).and Mary McDonald.
John was born in Isle of Skye in Scotland and died there

**GENERATION EIGHT:**
David Lochland Kinneir (1626-1665) and Margaret Thirkland (1629-1670)
David was born in Scotland and died in Midlothia, Scotland

**GENERATION NINE:**
John DeKynner (1601) and Maude (1601)
John was born and died in Scotland

**GENERATION TEN:**
Simon DeKynner (1577) and unknown wife
Born and died in Scotland

**GENERATION ONE:**
James Leslie England and Mary McKinney
*See above England genealogy for their information

**GENERATION TWO:**

**William Akin McKinney and Mary Jane Reynolds**
(1847-1923) Decatur Co, TN  and 1856-1945
William fought in the Civil War as a private. Pvt Co E 7 Regt
Tenn Cav Confederate States Army.

Their Children:

Willie (1876)
Annie C. (1878) born and died in Decatur Co, TN
James W. (1880) born and died in Decatur Co, TN
Charles L. (1883) born and died in Decatur Co, TN
Lura M. (1885) born and died in Decatur Co, TN
**Mary E. (1888) - my great grandmother married James L. England**
Lina E. (1891) born and died in Decatur, Co, TN
Henry Reynolds (1895-1948) born in Decatur Co, TN, married Jane Margaret Weatherly *see
pic below
Claude (1898-)born and died in Decatur Co, TN
Murtle (1900) born and died in Decatur Co, TN
Jewel (1900) born and died in Decatur Co, TN
Lee (1904) born and died in Decatur Co, TN

Mary McKinney's parents – William McKinney and Mary Jane Reynolds

Mary McKinney England's mother – Mary Jane Reynolds

Henry McKinney

## GENERATION THREE:

### William McKinney and Rebecca
(1811-1880) born in North Carolina / South Carolina (Chester), moved to Henderson Co., TN and died in Arkansas
Rebecca was born 1819 in SC and died 1881 in AK. In 1880 they lived in Hardin County, TN. At the time Anson County, NC became Chesterfield, SC.

Their Children:

> Mary E.G. (1836) born in SC
> James H. (1839-) born in SC
> John (1841) born in SC
> David John (1843) born in SC
> Susannah K. (1844) born in SC
> **William Akin (1847-1923) married Mary Jane Reynolds**
> Reuben G. (1849) born in SC
> Thomas J.A. (1851) born in SC
> Nancy Isabella (1855-1929) born Chester, SC, died in Arkansas

## GENERATION FOUR:

### William McKinney (1755-1842) and Mary Carter (1775-1840)
Born and died in Chester, SC and Mary born and died in Chester SC
Mary's parents were Alexander Carter and Annie Minskipe. Her father was born in Virginia.

Their Children:

> Alexander (1811-1896) born in Chesterfield, SC / died in Bradley, AK
> **William (1811-1880) born in SC, died in AK**
> Susannah (1812-1904) born and died in Chester, SC
> Mary Elizabeth (1815-1884) born and died in SC
> Jane (1821-1895) born and died in Chester, SC

** My Turnage relatives were also from Chester, SC

## GENERATION FIVE:

### William McKinney and Barbara Culp
(1729-1785) Born in Rariten, NJ and died in Chester, SC
Barbara Culp (1733-1790) born in Bucks, Pennsylvania and died in Chester, SC.
Married in 1752 in Craven, SC. Barbara's parents were Hans Casper Kolb and Alcordas Phillis. Her parents were from Swartzenau, Palatinate Germany. Her father died in Charleston, SC.

Their Children:

Nancy (1745) born and died in South Carolina
John (1753-1770)born in Chester, SC and died in Monroe, Mississippi
Mordecai (1753-1828)
**William (1775-1842)born and died in Chester, SC married Mary Carter**
Henry (1756-1813) born in Craven, NC married Temperance Jordan
Henry (1757-1758) died as infant
Hannah (1761-1839) born in Chester, SC and died in TN / married John Stedman
Mary (1767-1856) born and died in Fishing Creek, Chester, SC / married Ralph
    McFadden
James (1768-1844) born in Chester, SC and died in Carroll, TN / married Elizabeth
    Hamilton


## THE STORY OF WILLIAM McKINNEY AND BARBARA CULP

### BARBARA CULP
(Daughter of Hans Casper Culp)

Barbara Culp was born in Pennsylvania in 1733, the second daughter of Hans Casper Culp. Her date of death in present Chester County, SC is not known, but sometime after 1782, when she was named as administrator in her husband's will. She is buried in Old Richardson's Church, or Burnt Meeting House Cemetery, beside her husband, both graves unmarked.

She married William McKinney, born 1729 in Virginia, died 4/17/1785.
Barbara Culp (of German extraction) became one of the early frontier heroines. In August of 1761, she was attached by a group of sixteen Cherokee Indians while she was milking the cows during the absence of the McKinney men on a journey to Camden, South Carolina.  It is said that she probably would have been killed outright had it not been for the protection of two huge dogs which had accompanied her to milk.  As it was, she was scalped and left for dead with a tomahawk driven into her head.  Later regaining consciousness, she crawled to a nearby spring and washed her head in cold water.  Family history records that she completely recovered except for a tendency to "head colds."  The tomahawk used in the attack was kept as a memento of the near fatal incident until it was lost many years later.  H. B. Evans

She miraculously survived to bear more children. There have been many pages written into history books about the incident, but the best by far is in Elizabeth F. Ellett's WOMEN OF THE AMERICAN REVOLUTION, Vol III. That account was written by Daniel Green Stinson (1793-1879), the great histographer of Chester Co, SC.

After Barbara's horrible experience, she wore black silken caps to hide her baldness and wounds. My late great grandmother, Margaret McFadden Edwards, a great granddaughter of Barbara's, owned one of those caps, but its whereabouts is now unknown.


### WILLIAM MCKINNEY

He was a brother of James McKinney and both had come to present Chester County from Virginia. In youth, the two brothers had been hired by a horse drover to help drive horses to

South Carolina. Later, they entered into the business on their own and finally settled on Fishing Creek.

William McKinney's father was a Scotsman that had come to America from England and settled in Virginia. William McKinney seems to have been a very highly educated man and he became a much sought after legal advisor of the area, a "backwoods lawyer," when the closest such was in Charlestown, some two hundred miles and a week away. His name is found in many deeds and estates of the area and, in fact, many of the originals were penned by him. The home he built on Fishing Creek was marked on old maps as close to (Upper) Fishing Creek Presbyterian Church and the home stood until after the middle of this century when it was demolished for building material.

On 11 August 1774, William McKinney bought 100 acres of land from Christopher Strait that included the church, adjacent to the former land of Hans Casper Culp, so he actually owned the most famous landmark of Chester County today!

When William McKinney wrote his will, he named six children, but also named "my two youngest children" in such a manner it is not possible to determine if they were included in the named six. [This comes from "Captain Bill Book III" by Robert J. Stevens.....page 163-4]

William was hired to a horse drover who took horses to South Carolina. Later he carried horses to South Carolina and sold them on his own account. He finally settled in SC and purchased a tract of land about a mile west of Fishing Creek, nine miles from Chester village, the county seat of Chester Dist. They lived on a large farm with a very large spring on it in Craven, South Carolina.

In a deed dated September 9, 1771 in Chester District, James and Agnes Ferguson sold 140 acres to William McKinney on the north side of Fishing Creek. Apparently they had bought or obtained land in SC. The 140 acres sold were part of a land grant of 30 acres on Fishing Creek to James Ferguson dated December 12, 1768. In 1773 William McKinney lease to Henry Culp. On 8 February 1775 the Rev. John Simpson recorded in his visitations book that he had visited Wm. McKinney, his wife Barbara, and children John, William and Hannah. Also noted are visits to Barbara's brothers Augustin and Henry Culp.

William died on 27 April 1785 in Chester, South Carolina. When William McKinney wrote his will, he named six children, but also named "my two youngest children" in such a manner it is not possible to determine if they were included in the named six.


**THE WILL OF WILLIAM MCKINNEY WHO OWNED LOTS OF LAND IN SC**

*Will of William McKinney In the name of God Amen. Twentieth Day November One thousand Seven hundred and eighty two. I William McKinney, being through the mercy of God calling the mind the uncertainty of this life do make, constitute and ordain this my last will and testament and desire that it may be received by all as such I have my body to the earth from whence it was taken to be buried in a Christian decent manner at the discretion of my Executors herein after named.*

*I leave my soul to Almighty God my Creator and to Jesus Christ my Redeemer and to the Holy Ghost my satisfier, begging their most glorious acceptance of me, a returning penitent sinner. As concerning my worldly estate which it hath pleased God to bestow upon me I leave a bequest in the following manner. I leave and to my sons John and William, the house and plantation I now live on containing three hundred and fifty acres be is less or more I leave to my sons James and Henry three hundred and fifty acres, being parts of three tracts to be equally divided between them. Likewise, I leave by daughter Hanna one hundred and fifty acres of land likewise forth acres be it less or more of the lower end of the place bought of Edw. White the line is to begin at the creek at the mouth of the Spring Branch.*

*Likewise I will that my wife may have the benefit of the lower plantation left to Ja. And Henry during her life and the use benefit and command of the Negroes during her life and after her decease the three oldest Negroes is to be given to John, Wm., and Hannah I leave to my daughter Mary a Negro wench called Min to be given her at the age of twenty one my sons Henry is to have the increase of the Negro wench till Mary is of age. I leave to my sons Jas. A Negro boy to be given at the age, Likewise I leave to sons Henry, a young Negro child, Fawn, Likewise I will and desire that at the decease of my wife the one half of my cattle and moveable effects to be given to my two youngest children and the other half is to be given to or equally divided between John, Wm. Hannah, and Mary Likewise I constitute appoint my wife and my sons John, my lawful Ex'rs of this my last will and testament in witness my hand and seal the day and year above first written.*

*Wm. McKinney, his mark. Signed, sealed, and delivered in the presence of us, W., Willey, John McKinney, John Stuard. Recorded in Will Book AI, Page 198, Apt. 129, Pkg, 5059. State of South Carolina, County of Richland, Personally appeared before me Gertrude Foster who being duly sworn deposes and says that the above article or statement is true and correct, and that no part has been altered or changed in any way. Gertrude Foster, This 17th day Sept. 1938, Floride P. Goddard, Notary Public for South Carolina.*

## GENERATION SIX

**John Mordecai McKinney (1685-1760) and Marietje Sebring (1685-1760)**
He was born in Isle of The Skye, Scotland (or USA), lived in Pennsylvania and New Jersey and died in Lebanon, NJ.

Marietje Sebring was born 1685 in Bergen, Geneese, NJ and died 1760 in NJ. Her parents were Jan Roelofse Sebring and Adrianna Polhemus.
Her father was born in Drenthe Netherlands. Her mother was born in Ithamarca, Brazil.

Their Children:

John (1714-1772) born in Somerset NJ and died in Sunbury, NC.

William (1715-1777)born in Somerset, NJ and died in Warren, NJ

Daniel (1717-1808) born and died in NJ. Married Margaret Coffey. His grandson

Archibald was the one who started the McKinney Fort in Ky..

Jacob (1719-1776)born in Somerset, NJ and died in White Plains, Maryland

Annetje Ann (1721-1784) born in NJ, married William Scott

David (1725-1784) born in NJ, died in PA, married Rachel Long and Rebecca Lane

Mordecai (1727-1782)born in NJ, died in Dauphin, PA, married Agnes Bodyn

**William (1729-1785) married Barbara Culp**

Matthew (1731-1770) born in NJ

Kain (1733-1770) born in NJ

Daniel (1740-1809) born in Somerset, NJ, died in Lincoln, KY

**GENERATION SEVEN:**

**John Cullen McKinney (1650-1745) and Agnes Lander (1654-1733).and Mary McDonald.**
John was born in Isle of Skye in Scotland and died there.
Agnes was born and died in Scotland.

Children of **John Cullen McKinney** and **Mary Elizabeth McDonald** are:
John Dhu Mckinney, b. 1685, Scleofsky, Isle Skye, Scotland, d. 20 May 1760, Lebanon, Hunterdon, New Jersey, USA.

**John Mordecai McKinney**, b. 1672, Isle Skye, Scotland, d. 05 Dec 1760, Lebanon Township, Hunterdon, New Jersey, USA.

Mordecai McKinney, b. 1672, Isle Skye, Scotland, d. 12 May 1760, Lebanon, Hunterdon, New Jersey, USA[234].

Alexander McKinney, b. 1680, Isle Skye, Scotland, d., New Jersey, USA.

Robert Matthews McKinney, b. 1680, Scotland.

Susan Ann McKinney, b. 1680, Scotland.

Mary Elizabeth McKinney, b. 1680, Scotland.

William McKinney, b. 1682, Scotland.

Children of **John Cullen McKinney** and **Agnes Lander** are:

James Collin McKinney, b. 1680, Argylshire, Scotland, d. 09 Nov 1756, Londonderry, New Hampshire, USA.

Kain McKinney, b. 1680, Scotland, d., Virginia, USA.

Mordecai McKinney, b. 1685, Bergen, Genesee, New Jersey, USA, d. 20 May 1760, Lebanon, Hunterdon, New Jersey, USA

Thomas Mc Kinney, b. 1692, Scotland

## GENERATION EIGHT

**David Lochland Kinneir (1626-1665) and Margaret Thirkland (1629-1670)**
David was born in Scotland and died in Midlothia, Scotland.
His wife Margaret was born and died in Scotland. Her father was Lancelot Threlkeld.

Their Children:

John Cullen McKinney (1650-1745)

## GENERATION NINE

**John DeKynner (1601) and Maude (1601)**
John was born and died in Scotland.

Their Children:

**David Lochland Kinneir**

## GENERATION TEN:

Simon DeKynner (1577) and unknown wife

## ** THERE ARE A FEW GENERATIONS IN HERE THAT ARE UNIDENTIFIED BETWEEN SIMON AND WILLIAM DEKYNNER**

## FINAL GENERATION:

**William DeKynner born 1165 and died in 1214**

In the year 1165, King William granted to one William* De Kyner, a tract of land in St. Andrews Parish, County of Fife, Scotland, known as Kyner, or "Kyner Place," the first transfer of this land was to Symon De Kyner, in 1213 ; and the next to his son of the same name; in 1234; it was next transferred to John Kenner, in 1286, and next to his son of the same name, he held it until 1390.

One David Kenneir, was the owner in 1534, he appears to have been a man of considerable prominence in Scotland, and was elected to Parliament in 1560; he died June 21, 1584, aged 63 years.

In remote times, the name Kinnaird was found in the Scottish counties of Stirling, Farfar, Aberdeen and Perth. The name derived from "Caennard", a local place name signifying "the high head".

William de Kyner, first of the family of Kinney of whom there is an authentic record, lived during the reign of William I "The Lion" of Scotland, 1165 to 1214, and in the records of the famous abbey of Balmerino, in Fifeshire, near Dundee is mentioned as the proprietor of extensive lands under the abbey jurisdiction. This abbey was named from the ancient village of Balserynach, established by Queen Ermengarde, wife of William the Lion.

Descendants of William de Kyner were for generations residents of Balmerino and benefactors of the abbey, two of them serving as commendetators.

Simon de Kyner, the son of William made several grants of land to the abbey as did William's grandson Sir John de Kynner, in 1286.

David Kinnier, "of-the-ilk" the eighth in succession from William, was the bailie to the abbot of Balmerino

# LITTLE

# FAMILY

# GENEOLOGY

**Jacob Little**
B: 28 Mar 1755 United States
M:
D: 8 Mar 1838 United States

**Isaac Little**
B: 1715 Virginia, United States
D: 11 Feb 1797 United States

**Pleasant Mary Brown**
B: 2 Jan 1735 United States
D: 1781 United States

**Jacob Little**
B: 1802 United States
M: 1832 United States
D: 1846 United States

**Mary Ann Herring**
B: 1836 United States
M:
D:

**David Liles Little**
B: 8 Jan 1836 North Carolina, USA
M: 25 Dec 1870
D: 24 Nov 1906 Tennessee, United States

**Francis Liles**
B: 15 Feb 1814 United States
M: 1832 United States
D: 1895 Tennessee, United States

**William Scott Little**
B: 6 Mar 1879 Sardis, Cocke, Tennessee, Unite
M:
D: 3 May 1960

**Elizabeth Watts Totty**
B: 1833 Tennessee, United States
M: 25 Dec 1870
D: Feb 1925 Tennessee, United States

**William Little**
B: 1640 Massachusetts, USA
M:
D: 1700 Virginia, USA

**Thomas Little**
B: 1610 Devon, England
D: 12 Mar 1672 United States

**Anna Warren**
B: 1612 Greenwich, Kent, England
D: 19 February 1675 United State

**William Little**
B: 1660 United States
M: 1680 Virginia, United States
D: 1740 Virginia, United States

**Frances Raynor**
B: 1638 United States
M:
D: 1720 Virginia, United States

**William Little**
B: 1685 Surry, Virginia, United States
M: 1710 Surry, Virginia, United States
D: 1 Mar 1756 United States

**Elizabeth Church**
B: 26 Mar 1665 United States
M: 1680 Virginia, United States
D: 1691 Virginia, United States

**Isaac Little**
B: 1715 Surry, Surry, Virginia, United States
M:
D: 11 Feb 1797 Pitt, North Carolina, United Sta

**Morning Kimborough**
B: 1705 Surry, Virginia, United States
M: 1710 Surry, Virginia, United States
D: 1 Mar 1756 Virginia, United States

**Geoffrey Little Lyttell**
B: 1550
M:
D: 1626

**ROBARTE Lytell Lytle LYTTELL**
B: 1567 Barnstaple, Devon, England
M: 24 May 1592 Devonshire, England
D: 1600 England

**Jennifer Gifford**
B: 1550
M:
D: abt 1630 Devon, England

**Ephraime Little**
B: 1583 Devon, England
M: 1608 England
D: 12 Mar 1672 England

**DUENS SERREL**
B: 1571 Barnstaple, Devon, England
M: 24 May 1592 Devonshire, England
D: 1630 Barnstaple, Devon, England

**Thomas Little**
B: 1610 Devon, England
M: 19 Apr 1633 Plymouth, Plymouth, Massachu
D: 12 Mar 1672 Marshfield, Plymouth, Massach

**Elizabeth Jouatt**
B: 1583 Nayland, Suffolk, England
M: 1608 England
D: 12 Oct 1673 United States

These are my "Little family" relatives.

Jimmie England, daughter of James L. England and Mary McKinney married Clyde Little. They had children Tim, Stan, Pat Little. Jimmie was the postmaster of Sardis for many years. She was a kind and loving woman. She played on the Women's basketball team in school.

Opal England , daughter of James L. England and Mary McKinney married Aubert Little. They had sons Larry, Gary, Budgy. Opal also played on the women's basketball team in school.

The Little family goes back to the beginnings of Plymouth, Massachusetts from England. They also lived in Surry, VA, Pitt County, NC and Henderson County, Sardis, TN.

## GENERATION ONE:
Jimmie England and Clyde Little (1906)

And Opal England and Aubert Little (1909)

## GENERATION TWO:

### William Scott Little (1879-1960) born in TN
Sarah Imogene Carter Little (1882-1947)

He served in the military in 1898. He enlisted for the Spanish American War. In 1901 he was Deputy Coroner in Henderson Co. TN. W.S. Little posted as Deputy Coroner sometime in the 1901-1903 period.

Sarah Iomegene Carter was 1/4 Cherokee. So the Little descendants after her have Indian blood.

Their Children:

    Aubert Little (1908-1996) married Opal England.

    Had children: Larry, Gary, Jimmy ("Budgy"). Aubert worked for the county doing bulldozing and working with road machinery. He also worked for the prison in Ft. Pillow in Henning, TN.

    Clyde Little (1905-1949) married Jimmie England.
    Their Children: Stan, Tim, Pat.
    Clyde was in the cattle business – buying and selling cattle through several states. He was also a part time auctioneer. My Great Uncle Bill England (son of James L. England and Mary McKinney) worked with Clyde in the cattle business.

    Fay Little (1904) married William Clarence Shirley

Mabel Little (1902) married Grady Henry Montgomery and also married a Gilbert

Mabel Claire Little

**GENERATION THREE:**

**David Liles Little (1836-1906) Born in Anson County, NC**
died in Sardis, TN. He was married to Angeline Ann Presson and Elizabeth Watts.

Children with Angeline Presson (all born in Benton Co, TN (Camden)

Tranquilla Little (1854-1862) died of Diphtheria

John Bradford Little (1856-1947) married Mary Jane died in Oklahoma

> John B. Little was born on 16 May 1856 in Benton Co. TN to David Liles Little and Angeline Presson. For many years, J.B. was the pastor of the Little Flock Church, a Primitive Baptist Church located at Crossroads Ark. Like many of the Littles, J.B. was a prolific letter writer, with the subject usually relating to religion. Besides his extensive letters, J.B. wrote, typeset, and published a religious journal where he espoused his beliefs and argued his case in a long-standing argument with some of the church members.

> John B. Little was married to Mary Jane Ross on 26 Sep 1875 in Henderson Co. TN. Mary Jane Ross was born on 16 Jan 1859 in Henderson Co. TN. To Douglas Ross and Penelope Moore. She died on 16 Jan 1946. Mary Jane was a happy person who enjoyed life and could often be heard singing to herself while she worked. At her funeral service Grandpa looked down at Grandma in the casket and said, "Now, Mary, you can sing!" They were both buried in Coop Prairie Cem, Mansfield AR.

Martha Frances Little (1858-1943) died 1943 in Williamson, IL

Alvin Harvey Little (1861-1890) died in Nashville AK– killed by a car

Minerva Little (1862-

Sarah Little (1863-1865) died of Diphtheria

David Theopholis Little (1866-1876) died of Diphtheria

Aquilla Little (1868-1876) died of Diphtheria

Children with Elizabeth Watts Totty (children born in Henderson Co, TN)

Robert (1864-)

Charles P. (1874-1963)

Mary Luella (1878-1959)

**William S. (1879-1960) William Scott who married Sarah Imogene Carter**

Minnie Jane (1872-1976)

Lily Pearl (1883-1956)

Davy Liles Little

David Liles Little, son of Jacob and Frances, was born in Anson Co. in 1836. He moved with his parents, Jacob Little and Frances Liles to Benton Co. TN about 1846. He lived in Carroll, Benton Co., and Henderson Co. TN before moving to Illinois. In 1874 he returned to Tennessee and resided in Sardis, Henderson Co. until his death in 1906. A family story as to why the Little's moved to Henderson Co. (or perhaps IL) concerns David's killing a man who burned his gin in Benton County. It is supposedly borne out by early records of Hollow Rock Primitive Church (Benton CO) which stated that in April 1863 D.L. Little was excluded from the church "for misbehavior" for shooting Thomas Presson. However, we have been unable to locate these records.

David Liles Little died on 24 Nov 1906 in Sardis, Henderson Co. TN and was buried in a grave north-south, at Sardis Cemetery. He expressed a wish to be buried crossways, for he said he "had lived crossways with the world." A different version of the burial deals with the North-South conflict. Great grandson Wayne Little told that Jacob had made a pact with an old friend, Mr. Parker in Benton Co. TN, that each was to be buried with his head to the south, his feet to the north so, on Judgment Day, he could kick the behinds of the northern soldiers as they went back home.

Source: http://users.hal-pc.org/~happy/little/jacob01.html

Among the first settlers was Mr. D. L. Little, who became quite a noted nurseryman. He had a horse named Roscoe. In 1876, tragedy struck his family in the form of diphtheria. Four of his children, between the ages of one and thirteen, died of it. When the first child died, Mr. Little sent a son to get a preacher to hold the child's funeral. Then the son he had sent for the preacher took diphtheria and died before the preacher could return home. He held this child's funeral also. Within a few days, two more children died of diphtheria.

Jack Little, a grandson of D. L. Little, tells us that the dirt on the first grave wasn't dry when the fourth one was buried.

Mr. Little was a versatile man. He was a nurseryman and also wrote poetry. He expanded his nursery and established a branch in Lexington, Tennessee. This branch was operated by Flavial Azbill. He enjoyed poetry and wrote poetry, which he used on his shipping tags and in his ads. The following is an example:

> I'm sure these trees will surely please,
> The people of the West
> Cause Little knows and only grows
> The very, very best.

This little incident gives a little more insight into his character:

One morning he remarked to his new daughter-in-law that he was going out to put a rose bush in a bare spot in the pasture. She asked why he wanted to waste his time putting a rosebush off in a pasture. He replied, "Why Maudie, it will be just like meeting an old friend every time I go through the pasture."

Mr. Little and a Mr. Hinkle rode horseback and carried magnolia trees from his nursery to set out at Shiloh National Park. Jack Little says they are the ones at the entrance to the cemetery. (SOURCE: Sardis website : http://www.tnyesterday.com/books/sardis/sar-til.html) and From Beulah Hanna and Carra Holland, *History of Sardis, Tennessee*, Sardis Homecoming '86 Committee, May 1986.)

Here's an Advertisement from The Little Nursery:

D. L. Little Ad

# HOME NURSERIES

**A 100,000 FOR THE USUAL PRICE OF 25,000.**

## At Sardis and Lexington, Tenn.

Forty years testing varieties in West Tennessee has enabled the
senior proprietor to offer the very best varieties of

## FRUIT AND ORNAMENTAL TREES,

### At Remarkably Low Prices.

☞ Single or club orders promptly filled, and forwarded by
freight or express. Smaller packages by mail to any office in
the United States.

Say, will you come or send for trees
At early planting time?
Remember, they will surely please—
Dear friends, fall into line.
In forty years we've learned to grow
Such sorts as suit your climate best,

To leave off worthless sorts you know
Except enough to prove the test.
Now come, or send, without delay;
Now plant, and prove it as we say.

AGENTS WANTED. Address

### D. L. LITTLE,
Proprietor Home Nurseries,
**Sardis, Tennessee.**

The greatest men on earth have loved
To cultivate their fruits and flowers;
The great I AM of heaven above
Makes sweet to them such well spent hours.

The greatest Book begins, we see,
By pointing out this gift to man.
It ends with Everlasting Tree,
With Fruits forever there on hand.          D. L. L.

**GENERATION FOUR:**

**Jacob Little (1802-1846)  Anson Co, NC**
Frances Liles (1814-1895)

Their Children:

Nancy Nowell (1833-1915) married Matthew Presson

**David Liles Little (1836-1906) married Elizabeth Watts Totty /**

Ellen Little (1838-1914) died in Carbondale, IL married  Christopher Presson

Harvey Ingram (1839-1906) died in Echo, Ak married Lydia Ann Hunter

Miles Washington (1842-1920) born in NC, died in AK married Elizabeth Ann Cole

Edna Edney Little (1843) born in Anson, NC

Daniel J. (1846-1919) born in Camden, TN, died in AK married Sarah Gurley


**GENERATION FIVE:**

**Jacob Little (1755 in Surrey Co, VA and died in 1838 in Anson, NC)**
Mary Ann Herring

Jacob LITTLE who was born on 28 Mar 1755 in Surry Co. VA and moved with his family shortly thereafter to what is now Pitt Co. NC. Several Little families who may have been related lived in Surry Co. pre-1755 and in Pitt Co. after 1755 and can be found in numerous Pitt Co. deeds. Frequently appearing along with the Little's (Isaac, Pleasant, Jacob, James, Joseph) are Mooring and Knox.

In 1795, according to his Revolutionary War pension application, Jacob moved to Anson Co. NC in 1795. On August 7, 1795, as shown in Anson Co. Deeds, he obtained a land warrant for 100 acres on Gourdvine Creek. On Nov. 10, 1796, Jacob entered 100 acres on Gourdvine Creek, bordering Richard Lee's survey, and 100 ac on waters of Bridge Branch. At the same time, Isaac Little entered 100 acres on Gourdvine Creek bordering Richard Lee's land on the south side of the creek. It seems likely that Isaac and Jacob were brothers and had moved together from Pitt Co. to Anson Co. Another likely brother, Pleasant Little, joined them on Gourdvine in 1808.

Jacob's pension application was never accepted, and in 1855, Pleasant Menon Little, one of the children of Jacob Little, made another attempt to claim the pension. Jacob had died in March of 1838, leaving a will which mentioned his daughter Rebecca, son Jacob, and other unnamed daughters. His two sons Isaac and Hosea were executors. The sale of Jacob's land by Isaac and Hosea was witnessed by P.M. Little and Patrick Little, who we believe to be another son of Jacob.

Their Children:

        Hosea Little (1792-1850)

        Pleasant Minon (1800-1885)

        Jacob (1802-1846)

        Patrick (1805-1847)

        Rebecca Little (1837-1897)


## GENERATION SIX:

**Issac Little (1715-1797) and Pleasant Mary Brown (1735-1781)**
born in Surrey Co, VA, lived in Pitt Co, NC.

Their Children:

        James (1742-1855)

        Jacob (1755-1838)

        James (1755-1855)

        Penelope (1758-

        Pleasant (1762-1832)

        William Franklin (1764-1826)

        Elisha (1767-

        Isaac (1774-1830)

## GENERATION SEVEN:

**William Little (1685-1756) Surrey, VA to Beaufort, NC**
and Morning Kimborough (1705-1756)

Their Children:

        Jeannett (1713-1764)

        Abraham (1715-1798)

        Isaac (1715-1797) married Pleasant Mary Brown

John (1715-1755)

William (1724-1794)

Jane Morning (1728-)

Isaac (1730-1824)

Jacob (1735-1791)

Pleasant Minon (1800-1797)

## GENERATION EIGHT:

**William Little (1660-1740) born in Massachusetts, married in Surrey, VA and died in Surry, VA**

Elizabeth Church (1665-1691) married in 1680
also married to Martha Parnell in 1692

**Children with Elizabeth Church:**

William (1685-1756) married Mourning Kimbrall

**Children with Martha Parnell:**

Thomas (1692-1676)

Martha (1696-

John (1699-1769)

Thomas (1715-1748)

## GENERATION NINE:

**William Little (1640-1700) born in Plymouth, MA, died in Surry, VA**
Frances Raynor (1638-1720)

Children:

William (1660-1740)

**GENERATION TEN:**

**Thomas Little (1610-1672) born in Devon, England, married in 1633 in Plymouth, MA, died in** Plymouth, MA
Anna Warren (1612-1675)

Their Children:

      Thomas Little (1609-1672)
      Abigail (1635-1660)
      Patience (1635-1720)
      Hannah (1635-1710)
      Ruth (1636-1675)
      WIlliam (1640-1700)
      Mercy (1645-1693)
      Samuel (1645-1699)
      Isaac (1646-1699)
      John (1647-1725)
      Ephraim (1650-1717)
      Thomas (1655-1676)
      Ruth (1660-
      Patience (1662-

**LITTLE, THOMAS-**

Thomas Little first appears in Plymouth records on the
1633 tax list. On 19 April 1633 he married Ann Warren, daughter of
Mayflower passenger Richard Warren and his wife Elizabeth (PCR 1:13). On
7 October 1633 Little sold his dwelling house to Richard Higgins for
twenty-one bushels of corn (PCR 1:16). On 28 May 1635 he made a gift of
land to his brother-in law Robert Bartlett (PCR 1:34). On 12 March
1638/39 William Taylor (son of William Taylor of Boddington, County
Cornwall, carpenter) transferred his indenture with the consent of all
from Mr. John Atwood to Thomas Little (PCR 1:119).

Little moved to Marshfield, where he became constable on 3 June 1662 (PCR 4:15). He
bought farm land in Marshfield which had belonged to Maj. William
Holmes, deceased, and on 3 June 1662 the court ordered that in view of
his many improvements of the land, if anyone should show better title in
the future, such person would have to pay him fully for his improvements
(PCR 4:16). On 9 June 1665 he was fined l/10 pound for not keeping
secret the proceedings of the grand jury, of which he was a member (PCR
4:101). When he refused to pay rents claimed by Mrs. Rachel Davenport
for the land of the late William Holmes, the court on 1 May 1666 awarded
her 15 pounds, which, because of his improvements, was less than she had
claimed (PCR 4:119). On 14 August 1672 administration of the estate of
Thomas Little of Marshfield was given to his widow, Anna Little (PCR
5:101). His will dated 12 May 1671, inventory 4 April 1672, mentioned

his wife; his sons Isaac, Ephraim, Thomas, and Samuel; his grandson John Jones; and his servant Sarah Bonney (MD 4:161). His son Thomas died in King Phillip's War at Rehoboth, and in his will (MD 4:164) we learn that his father Thomas also had daughters Ruth, Hannah, Patience, and Mercy. The younger Thomas died without having married. The senior Thomas Little also had a daughter Abigail, who married Josiah Keene and predeceased her father (MD 8:191-92, 19:128, 28:5-6).
Source: Plymouth Colony Its History & People 1620-1691 by Eugene Aubrey Stratton

First Pioneers of Marshfield, MA (see Thomas Little on left side)

Fig. 4: Joined chest, attributed to Thomas Little (in MA by 1630–1672), Marshfield, Ma, 1680–1720. Red oak, pine, iron hardware. H. 27, W. 52, D. 20 in. Courtesy of the Isaac Winslow House, Marshfield, Ma. Descended in the Little family of Marshfield through Mary Little Winslow (1704–1772). Pine top may be replaced.

Thomas Little's Chest

## GENERATION ELEVEN:

**Ephraime Little (1583-1672)  Born and died in Devon, England**
Elizabeth Jouatt (1583-1673)

Their Children:

> Thomas (1610-1672)
> Anna Warren (1612-1675)
> Elizabeth (1617-1670)

## GENERATION TWELVE:

**Robarte Lytell Lytle (1567-1600) born in Barnstaple, Devon England**
Duens Serrel (1571-1630)

Their Children:

Ephraime Little (1583-1672)


**GENERATION THIRTEEN:**

**Geoffrey Little Lyttell (1550-1626)**
Jennifer Gifford (1550-1630)

Their Children:

      Robarte Lytell (1567-1600)

**OTHER BOOKS BY THIS AUTHOR, KATHERINE FLETCHER**

These books can be purchased through Amazon or with the website links below:

The Rice Family History – Dingle Ireland to VA, NC and West Tennessee
https://www.createspace.com/3536928


The Turnage Family History – England to VA, NC, SC and West Tennessee
https://www.createspace.com/3652300


Aunt Irene's Secret Southern Recipes – from the recipes of Irene England Holt
https://www.createspace.com/3646329

www.ingramcontent.com/pod-product-compliance
Lightning Source LLC
Chambersburg PA
CBHW041514280526
45792CB00004B/1245